MW01234981

Trading Strategies

Exploring The Best Day Trading + Forex Trading + Swing Trading +Futures Trading Strategies You Can Use To Make Money

By

Fabian Miller

TABLE OF CONTENTS

INTRODUCTION

Thank you very much for purchasing this book. An option is defined as a type of contract, sold by one party to another, that gives the option buyer the right, but not the obligation, to buy or sell the underlying stock at a predetermined price.

Options cannot exist indefinitely and each option has an expiration date. The buyer of the option of a specific option may have the right to exercise his option only when the option expires, or he may have the right to exercise the option at any time up to the expiration date (depending on whether the option follow the European or American convention).

Instead Forex trading has existed since civilization began, we just have to go back to 1944 so we can look at the origin of the current Forex structure.

After the Great Depression and the World Wars, world leaders tried to achieve some sort of stability in the economy and the first step was to work out a new financial and economic system. In this book you will find everything you need to become a true master and I am sure you will do great things.

Enjoy.

CHAPTER 1 - Different Existing Trading Styles According to Personal Taste and/or Available Portfolio

Forex Trading strategy is what forex traders do to buy or sell financial instruments at a given time to generate profits. Forex Trading strategies are nowadays done, either manually or automatically. A trader is using manual strategies when he or she interprets the trading signals and as a result, decides to buy or sell

Before choosing a Forex Trading strategy, it is important to identify which of these four trading styles fits your personality:

Day Trading

Day trading is a short-term trading style designed to buy and sell financial securities within the same trading day. That is closing all positions by the end of the trading day. In Day Trading, you can hold your trades for minutes or even hours. Day traders deal with financial instruments like options, stock, currencies, and contracts for difference. Many day traders are investment firms and banks. Day traders use technical analysis to make trading decisions.

Pros

- Day traders are not affected by unmanageable risks and negative price gaps because all positions are closed by the end of the trading day.

- There are a substantial number of trading opportunities

- Traders can be extremely profitable due to the rapid returns

Cons

- Traders can be extremely unprofitable due to the rapid returns

- You don't have to be concerned with the economy or long-term trends

- Huge opportunity cost

- Day traders have to exit a losing position very quickly, to prevent a greater loss.

Swing Trading

Swing trading is where a trader holds an asset between one and several days in an attempt to capture gains in the financial market. This type of traders doesn't monitor the screens all day, and they do it a few hours a day. Swing traders usually rely on technical analysis to look for trading opportunities.

Pros

- Swing traders can rely solely on technical analysis, which simplifies the process

- Requires less time to trade compared to day-trading

Cons

- Swing traders are exposed to overnight and weekend risks

- Generally, swing trading risks are as a result of market speculation

- It is difficult to know when to enter and exit a trade when swing trading

Scalping Trading

Scalping is the fastest trading style where traders hold positions for a very short time frame. Traders here gain profits due to small price changes. The scalpers hold a position for a short period to gain profits. Traders with large amounts of capital or bid-offers spread narrowly prefer scalping. Scalping follows four principles:

Small moves are more frequent - even when the market is quiet, scalpers can make hundreds or thousands of trades

Small moves are easier to obtain - small moves happen all the time compared to large ones

Less risky than larger moves - scalpers only hold positions for short periods therefore because they have less exposure the risk is also lower

Spreads can be both bonuses and costs. Spread is the numerical difference between the bid and ask prices. Various parties and different strategies view spread as either trading bonuses or costs.

Pros

- Positions can be liquidated quickly, usually within minutes or seconds
- Very profitable when used as a primary strategy
- It's a low-risk strategy
- Scalpers are not exposed to overnight risks

Cons

- Requires an exit strategy especially during large losses

- Not the best strategy for beginners; it involves quick decision-making abilities.

Position Trading

Position trading involves holding a position open for a long period expecting it to appreciate. Traders here can hold positions for weeks, months, or even years. Position traders are not concerned with short-term fluctuations; they are keener on long-term views that affect their positions. Position trading is not done actively. Most traders place an average of 10 trades a year.

This strategy seeks to capture full gains of long-term trading, which would result in an appreciation of their investment capital. Position traders use fundamental analysis, technical analysis, or a combination of both to make trading decisions. To succeed position, traders need plans in place to control risk as well as identify the entry and exit levels.

Pros

- Traders have a longer period to reap fruits.

- Trader's time is not on demand. Once the trade has been initiated, all they can do is wait for the desired outcome

Cons

- Traders may fall victim to opportunity costs because capital is usually tied up for longer periods.

- Position traders tend to ignore minor fluctuations, which can turn to trend reversals, a change in the price direction of a position.

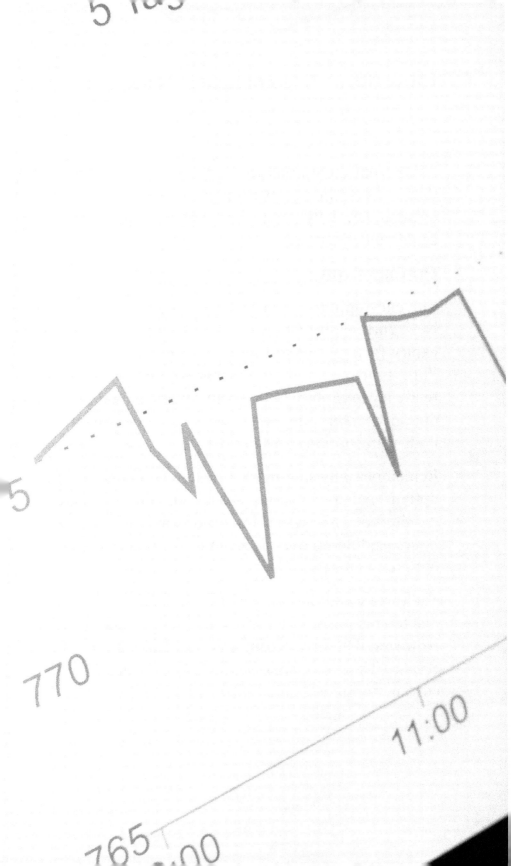

CHAPTER 2 - Important Daily Times and Events

Aside from the market interest and liquidity movement during worldwide forex trading day, you also need to be aware of key daily events that tend to happen around the same time every day.

Options Expiry

Currency options are usually set to expire either at the New York expiry (10 a.m. Eastern Time) or the Tokyo expiry (3 p.m. Tokyo time). The option expiry in New York is the more important expiry option since it has the tendency to capture both North American and European option market interest. Once an option expires, the underlying option stops to exist.

Remember, any spot market hedging done based on the option being suddenly alive should be carefully monitored. This trigger important price changes in the hours leading up to and just after the expiry time of the option.

The variety and the amount of currency option interest is just too big to suggest any one method to spot the prices. However, if you are getting some volatility around 10 am Eastern Time, this could be caused by the expiry of some currency options.

Establishing the Rate at Currency Fixtures

Currency fixing refers to a set time every day when the prices of currencies for business transactions are fixed or set.

There are scheduled currency fixtures in different financial centers around the world. However, the two most important are the London Time (4 p.m.) and the Tokyo Time (8:55 a.m.).

From a trading perspective, these fixtures may see a surge in a specific currency pair (usually 15 to 30 minutes) to the fixing time that suddenly ends precisely.

A sharp movement in a particular currency pair on fixing-related buying, for instance, may suddenly come to an end at the fixing time and see the price immediately drop back to where it was before.

Traditionally, the London Forex Fix is benchmarked to WM/ Reuters fixing rates.

Squaring Up on the Forex Futures Markets

One of the biggest futures markets in the world, the Chicago Mercantile Exchange (CME), offers forex futures through the International Monetary Market (IMM) subsidiary exchange. A forex futures contract specifies at which a specific currency can be purchased or sold in the future.

The trading of currency futures closes every day on the IMM at 2 p.m. central time (CT) or around 3 pm in the East Coast. Numerous traders in the futures market usually square up or close any open positions at the end of every trading session for margin requirements or to limit their exposure overnight. The last hour leading to the closing of the IMM usually creates a surge that spills over into the spot market.

Market liquidity is usually at the lowest in the afternoon in New York. This results in sharp movements in the futures market that can trigger volatility in the spot market around this period.

There's no easy way to tell if or how the IMM close will cause a movement in the spot market in New York, so you have to be aware of this.

The USD Index

The USD index is a futures contract that is listed in the New York Board of Trade (NYBOT) and Financial Instruments Exchange (FINEX) futures exchanges that is based in Dublin.

The dollar index refers to the average USD value against a basket of six other primary currencies. However, this is heavily weighted towards currencies in Europe.

Here are the specific weights of other currencies in the USD index:

✓ Swiss Franc (3.6%)

✓ Swedish Krona (4.2%)

✓ Canadian Dollar (9.1%)

✓ British Pound (11.9%)

✓ Japanese Yen (13.6%)

✓ Euro (57.6%)

Take note that the European currency share of the basket (Switzerland, Sweden, United Kingdom, and Eurozone) accounts for 77.3%.

USD is the most powerful currency today with the majority of forex trading normally involving the dollar on one side of the pair. Global commodities are valued in USD and numerous global currency reserves maintained by central banks are in USD.

It is not surprising that the USD is considered as the most liquid currency in the world.

As a day trader, you need to know if the USD is strong or weak. The USD index allows you to do this because it provides you a wider perspective of how the dollar is performing in the G10 forex space. As a forex trader, you should follow the USD index especially its technical developments.

Forex and Other Financial Instruments

While forex market is the largest financial market in the world in terms of daily trading volume, it is not the only financial instrument that you can trade. Aside from currencies, you can also trade gold, oil, and of course company equities or stocks.

You have probably heard about the supposed interconnectivity of forex to these financial instruments. Unfortunately, much of the information out there are not true at all and you should learn how to determine which one is true and which one is just pure hype.

Seasoned forex traders usually look for a link between two different financial instruments depending on individual circumstances. You must be careful in getting caught up in these "connections".

Even if there's an apparent connection between two instruments (moving in harmony or inversely against each other) it usually happens over the long term - months or even years. This connection usually provides minimal information on how the markets will connect in the short term, which is an important factor to consider if you are a forex day trader.

And even if two instruments are connected with each other in the short-term, there's no certainty if the correlation will persist in the long-term.

For example, depending on where you look at the performance of gold and USD (inverse connection) you may still find a correlation co-efficient (not less than -0.2 and not more than -0.8). Remember, if you see a zero correlation in the charts, it means that the two instruments are not correlated at all.

Different financial instruments are traded in their own markets, so they behave in their own internal dynamics based on the market interest, trader positions, and significance of news.

There's a possibility that the financial markets might overlap and will demonstrate various degrees of correlation. And as a trader, it will help you if you are also aware of what is happening in other financial markets.

But you should look at each market in its own right and to have your own strategy and trading plan for each instrument.

For now, we can briefly discuss other important financial instruments and see their correlation with currencies.

Stocks

Stocks refer to the units of shares in the equities market. The movement in the stock market follow individual prospects for each company, sector or industry that you hold shares. On the other hand, currencies are much larger securities that usually fluctuate in response to various economic and political developments. Hence, there's minimal logic that the stock market is correlated to the forex market. Long-term correlation studies bear this out with the co-efficient of 0 between the main USD pairs and the stock markets.

There are some instances that the currencies and stocks cross each other, even though this is rare and for short-term only.

For example, when the equity market volatility peaks on (such as when S&P 500 loses higher than 2 per cent in a single trading day) the USD can also experience more tension than the usual. However, there's no way to predict this through correlation studies.

NASDAQ may dwindle down during an unexpected rise in interest rates, while the USD may even increase on the sudden surge.

Meanwhile, the Japanese stock market can be affected by JPY value mainly because of the significance of the export sector in the Japanese economy.

A sudden rise in the value of JPY may cause a negative response in the equities market because this would make exports more expensive and thus could affect the value of import sales.

Fixed Income Markets

Fixed income markets mainly trade bonds, wherein you are guaranteed an income within a specific time. The bond market has a more intuitive correlation to currencies compared to equities because the bonds and currencies are both significantly affected by interest rate movements.

However, the short-term market dynamics of supply and demand usually affects the efforts to establish a possible correlation between the two instruments for the short-term.

In some instances, the forex market could respond first based on the changes in interest rate movements. There are times that the bond market could reflect the changes in the expectations on the interest rate with the currencies trying to follow.

If you want to become a forex day trader, you should look at the current yields of government bonds on major currencies so you can monitor the possible changes in interest rates.

Gold

We have learned that gold was used by governments to back up the value of their currencies. While this is no longer the case today, gold is still used by investors and traders as a hedge against inflation and it is also a much more valuable alternative to the USD.

For the long term, the correlation between gold and USD is typically inverse. If the dollar is weaker, then gold is stronger. If the dollar is stronger, then gold is weaker.

But for the short term, the two markets have their own interest level and liquidity that makes the correlation between them too tedious.

Basically, the gold market is a lot smaller compared to the currencies. Thus, if you are also interested in trading gold, you should also monitor the movement of USD.

Robust movements in the price of gold can attract the attention of forex traders and typically affect the dollar inversely.

Oil

Some financial experts say that there's a correlation between oil and currencies especially JPY and USD. This is basically based on the premise that because some countries are oil-producing countries, their currencies are influenced by the oil price.

The assumption is, if a country is importing oil, then its currency is affected by the oil price fluctuations.

However, correlation studies show no clear link to back this up, especially in the short-term. If there's a correlation in the long-term, this is usually against the USD as much as more than any currency regardless if the country is importing or exporting oil.

Take note that oil is seen as an input to calculate inflation and also considered as a factor that can limit the general growth of a country's economy.

Higher oil price may lead to a higher inflation rate and the other way around. Because of the fact that the US is significantly reliant on energy, and also heavily driven by capitalism, it favors lower oil prices.

If you also want to speculate in the oil market while trading currencies, you need to consider the fluctuation in the oil prices when you look at growth projections and inflation of a certain country.

But remember, there are other factors that affect the overall financial markets, not only oil price.

CHAPTER 3 - Influencers of the Forex Markets

Any financial market is influenced by a wide array of factors. On the stock market, company news can drive an individual stock to new heights or make it since to new lows. A good jobs report can send the S & P 500 soaring, which means that most companies are going to see their stock rising. A trade deal gone bad can send things in the other direction.

Market Makers

A lot of Forex trading still goes on between banks. In the business, this is known as the interbank Forex market. It's done by computer now, but this is the same kind of trading that went on between the banks before the advent of the retail trading market created by the FX dealers. Market makers influence the Forex markets through interbank trading.

Every bank has a market maker. In fact, they have a market maker for all the majors. Hence, at the very least, the bank will have seven market makers, with each market major managing one of the major currency pairs. The job of the market maker is to set a price that the bank is willing to pay at the time for a given currency pair. Since banks deal with an enormous amount of currency compared to retail traders, any move made by a bank is going to have a huge influence on the exchange rates.

Through the market maker, they set the parameters for each of the major currency pairs. These are the market makers, in the truest sense of the word.

Of course, competition between banks helps dampen the impact. Different banks throughout the world have their own market makers and they will have their own buying and selling terms and they will have to meet in the middle in order to come to terms.

Each market maker operates from a starting point of bid and ask prices for their currency pair. They can make deals with other big players. Banks can do currency trading using credit terms, which magnifies the impact of their deals because they are much larger than they would be in cash.

Market makers can also be hedge funds or broker-dealers. These people set the rates on the retail markets where individual traders trade. While this sounds bad at first, it shouldn't put you off as far as entering trades. The reason is that there is not one market marker on the retail market. There are many market makers – remember that any FX dealer acts as a market maker. In the retail market, the market makers know they can attract more traders by having the best deals. This generates competition among the market makers, which can help individual traders get better deals.

One of the most important ways that the market makers help individual traders is by maintaining liquidity in the markets. That is, they ensure that when you want to enter a trade, you're able to do so and do it instantly. Moreover, broker-dealers acting as market makers can offer more favorable spreads, which means lower costs for you to enter the trade.

You might be asking at this point how the banks play a role here. Remember that the broker-dealers have to trade with the banks. It's important to keep the complete picture of the Forex market in your head. While the broker-dealers can trade directly with individual traders, or facilitate trading between individual traders, behind it, all the brokers are trading with the banks. That means the banks have a fundamental influence on what's going on. In other words, the banks are influencing things by the exchange rates that they are willing to accept in deals and so they influence the starting point for the brokers. That is going to set constraints on what the spreads are as well.

Political Factors and Foreign Affairs

There are so many factors that can influence the strength of currency; it's hard even to list them all. One thing that has always influenced currency prices relative to one another is the international situation. Since the end of World War Two, or even before, the dollar has been seen as the go-to international currency. People view the United States government as strong and immovable. Whether or not that is still justified is an open question, but that has been the perception and it continues in the present, at least for now.

A consequence of this is that if there is international trouble, people are going to look to move their money into dollars. One thing that is true all around the world is that people will accept dollars as payment. Do you see people clamoring in order to get their hands-on Chinese currency? Of course not. Who would want it? China might dream of a world where they have the reserve currency, but the reality is even now that's not anywhere near happening. The Chinese government is a totalitarian state and people don't trust them. That isn't to say the United States government is peaches and cream. That isn't the point – but the U.S. economy remains the largest and most stable in the world. The fact that China's currency isn't contained in any major trading pairs should tell you something.

If there is a war, then people will be moving their currency into U.S. dollars fast. God forbid, if a war happens during a time when you are Forex trader, you'd be smart to move to favor the US dollar in your trades.

Now let's be clear, we are talking about a major war where everyone's security is threatened, not some kind of "police action" like an invasion of Iraq. The United States doesn't have to be involved at all to cause a significant strengthening of the U.S. dollar. In recent years, China has been getting into lots of territorial disputes with its neighbors. Suppose for a moment that this turned into a "hot" war. A lot of friendly countries are in the area, including Australia, Japan and South Korea. They'd all feel very threatened, the dollar would immediately become stronger, as currency traders would be bidding up the price of dollars on the Forex markets.

Speaking of South Korea, that is something to watch as well. The North Koreans have settled down lately, but anything that leads to instability in the Pacific region or Europe bodes well for the US Dollar.

Inflation Rates

When you have low inflation rates, it helps your currency. Maybe to get a grip on this we can think about what doesn't help your currency. If you have really high inflation, it means it takes a lot more currency to buy the same goods than it took in the past. When inflation rates are high, the time periods over which money becomes worthless can be surprisingly short. While developed countries are more stable, high inflation rates can happen. In the late 1970s inflation rates in the United States skyrocketed. They weren't at Zimbabwe levels, but at 13-14% they made life in the US far more difficult than it would have been otherwise. Everyone also recalls that in the 1920s, Germany experienced out of control inflation. It was so bad that people had to use wheel barrels to carry huge amounts of cash around just to buy basic staples like coffee or a loaf of bread. Too bad credit cards hadn't been invented yet.

A high rate of inflation definitely weakens the value of a currency, but the real factor is the comparison of inflation rates between countries that are in a currency pair. If Europe had a 1% inflation rate, but Canada had a 10% inflation rate, that would favor the Euro over the Canadian dollar in currency trading, all other things being equal. Remember that a 10% inflation rate means that the purchasing power of the Canadian dollar would be dropping 10% a year so if you could buy 10 apples last year using one Canadian dollar, this year you could only buy nine.

And if you don't have as much purchasing power at home, you'd expect to buy less with Canadian dollars anywhere, which means you could also buy fewer Euros with them as well. Of course, some of this is just common sense, if Canada had high inflation, individual traders and banks around the world would be shying away from their desire to own Canadian dollars.

Interest Rates

The interest rates set by the central banks throughout the world can have an impact on the strength of currency as well. This can be related to inflation since central banks will raise interest rates in order to try and tamp down inflation. This also happened in the United States in the late 1970s, when the US Federal Reserve began raising interest rates to try and get inflation under control. Interest rates went as high as 18%, causing the media to create the "misery index."

But like inflation, when comparing two countries, it's the differences in interest rates that matter. Higher interest rates can help a country's currency strengthen. The reason for this is simple. People are always looking for a return on their money that is they want to make more money than they presently have. When interest rates are high, this can provide a lot of opportunities to make money while preserving capital at the same time. Therefore, if interest rates are higher in one country relative to another, it's going to attract investment dollars – that is foreign capital will start flowing into the country so that they can invest in anything that generates interest payments. It could be investing in bonds, real estate, or any asset that will result in interest payments. But guess what, if you want to invest in country AAA, you must convert your currency into the currency AAA. That's a higher demand for AAA, which means its value is going to rise relative to the country that is the source of the funds.

If the United States had high-interest rates, but Europe kept theirs artificially low, then money would flow from Europe to the United States to take advantage of the high-interest rates and this would drive up the value of the US dollar relative to the Euro.

Rising Government Debts

A high and rising government debt can weaken a currency over time. This happens because foreign investors are less interested in investing in a country that carries a large amount of debt. Government debt has an impact that can be said to "crowd out" investment. Again, everything is relative. The United States has let its debt get out of control over the past 10 years, so you would think that would be a negative. Maybe the Japanese Yen would end up being stronger relative to the dollar. However, Japan has let its government debt get out of control too so it's hard to see who has a favorable position relative to this one data point.

International Trade

A country that is importing a lot of goods can weaken its currency. If AAA is importing a lot of goods from BBB, that means BBB has to accept large amounts of payments in AAA currency, which they are going to have to sell in order to get their own currency back, or companies in AAA will trade for BBB currency in order to buy the goods with BBB currency.

2500
1.51 Sec
2,500
4,567
2,315
7,325
Link One
Link Eight
Daily active users
Daily active users
Daily active users
Top 5
Disbursement
Progress
Marketing
Media
Engagement
Awareness
30%
10%
20%
15%
123k
53k
23k
3k

CHAPTER 4 - Common Mistakes and Tips for Beginners in Forex Trading

The forex market due to its low restriction makes the market one of the most available market in the world. With an internet connection, phone or computer, and some few dollars, you can begin trading in the market. However, because of its free accessibility does not mean it is easy to make huge returns.

Common Forex Mistakes

Mistakes in forex are unavoidable but there are always remedies to deal with such a situation. Before you consider plunging into trading, it is important to consider the following mistakes and do everything possible to avoid them in the future. Most people are persuaded to venture into forex trading with fantasies of getting rich overnight.

Undeniably, the opportunities in the forex market are innumerable for you to make money and live the lifestyle you want. Notwithstanding, the forex road is not an easy road to travel because it is full of bumps. If there is anything, I can assure you as a beginner is that you will struggle for various reasons including having a poor forex foundation, poor trading structure, and impatience.

Tips for Trading Forex

Learning to trade successfully in the forex market is quite problematical for new traders. Most traders have the mindset of getting rich overnight, which is not something realistic. Forex trading can be prodigious particularly if you are a beginner and do not know the rules guiding the market. These tips will help you in your trading journey as a beginner. It is always advisable not to forget the basics because without them you will struggle in the market.

Pick your broker cleverly

If you can choose the right broker, then you are halfway done in the forex market. Before choosing any broker, it is important for you to review various brokers. Ensure to seek recommendations from professional traders and make your own research because some traders will recommend a particular broker because of their affiliate programs. Take your time as we have various fake brokers looking for traders like you to ripe off. Do not be moved by mouthwatering deals, rather look for an authorized broker with years of accomplishment.

Develop your strategy

A list of tips on forex trading is not complete without mentioning strategy. As a beginner, you need to create your own trading strategy that works for you. Every trader should know what to expect and get from the market. You should set a definite goal because it will help discipline yourself when trading.

Learn Slowly

Forex is not something you learn and stop over time. Every new skill requires consistent learning to grasp the basics. Additionally, you do not have to rush your learning process. Take your time slowly and begin by investing a little amount of money. Remember that slow and steady will win the race as a beginner.

Control your emotions

If you allow your emotions to guide you when trading, you will regret it later. I am not telling you that it is easy but you can control it. You need to stay rational in order to make wise choices during trading. If you let your emotions to rule over you, you are bound to expose yourself to pointless risks. Forex trading is risky but you can control the level of risk that can happen.

Do not trade if you are under stress

Hardly can you see someone who concentrates optimally when under stress. Traders who decide to do that will surely make an irrational decision, which will cost them money. Therefore, before thinking of trading, ensure to identify anything that will cause stress and eliminate them before it eliminates your forex account (do not mind me I am just joking but there is a sense to it). If you had a stressful day and still had to trade, consider taking a deep breath while allowing your mind to focus on what you are about to do. You can overcome stress in various ways such as exercising, sleeping, and listening to music, hanging out with friends. Whatever the situation is, find a solution to your stress and manage it effectively.

Never stop practicing
Do not neglect this tip because it is crucial to your success or failure as a forex trader. Hardly can you succeed on your first encounter in the forex market. Therefore, when you make your first mistake, do not relent because, with consistent practicing, you will be among the top traders. However, you have the adventure of using a demo account to perfect your skill.

Risk is part of the game
If you are not ready to risk, you are not ready for the forex market. Most brokers will advise you that trading is risky and you should accept that fact. If you think that in forex you are going to have a sweet ride, then you need a reality check. Additionally, I have seen mouthwatering advertisements promising you the "unpromising." Well, you should be realistic about your goals and strategies.

Patience is priceless
Do you remember the old adage? "True success is never instantaneous." That holds true in the forex market. It is the product of consistent planning and work, which many beginners tend to overlook. There is no easy path to making a profit in the market. Let patience have her way in you.

Upgrade your knowledge continuously
The more you trade, the more new things you learn. Improve your knowledge by looking at trends, analyzing news, and financial processes. Furthermore, do not neglect the fundamental basis you have learned. Significantly, you should study, practice, and continue this routine. A knife gets dull when it is left idle. Sharpen

your trading skill with continuous learning and practicing.

Take breaks

All work and no play make Jack a dull student. You can take routine breaks especially when you are under stress. For those glued to multiple computer winds to analyze data from various sources, it is important to take a break as you may feel pressured.

Trends are essential

Trends are important for any trader and you should not neglect them. The capability to identify these trends makes it a valuable investment for you. I understand there are various trends, it is important to ignore those that will lead to disaster. Trends give you a picture of what may come in the future. With this, you can prepare for the future.

Planning is a necessary ingredient

Forex trading is not sports betting where you gamble the team to win or score. Forex trading is a strategic game that requires painstaking planning and attention to evaluate your next move before taking action. Before starting any trade, formulate a plan that includes challenging questions like:

- What is my primary plan?

- What is plan B?

- What strategy should I employ?

- What are my loss and profit margins?

Understand the charts

You will trade in various markets and these require different information to analyze each trade. We have numerous tools you can use to make your trading easier. However, charts are time efficient and serve as the best option for beginners. You should not know them, only you should learn how to read and use them to your advantage.

Incorporate stop-losses in your trades

Setting stop-loss for trade is an efficient strategy to use when trading. With stop-loss, you minimize your risk and escape any trade that goes haywire. Additionally, avoid greediness by setting the maximum profit and loss range. Once you hit your target, you should avoid the trap of placing another trade.

CHAPTER 5 - Money Mistakes to avoid

Now we'll turn our attention to giving some tips, tricks and advice on errors to avoid in order to ensure as much as possible that you have a successful time trading.

- Avoid the Get Rich Quick Mentality

Any time that people get involved with trading or investing, the hope is always there that there's a possibility of the big winning trade. It does happen now and then. But quite frankly, it's a rare event. On many occasions, even experienced traders are guessing wrong and taking losses. It's important to approach Forex for what it really is. It's a business. It is not a gambling casino even though a lot of people treated that way so you need to come to your Forex business—and it is a business no matter if you do it part-time, or quit your job and devote your entire life to it—with the utmost seriousness. You wouldn't open a restaurant and recklessly buy 1 thousand pounds of lobster without seeing if customers were coming first. So, why would you approach Forex as if you were playing slots at the casino? Take it seriously and act as if it's a business because it really is. Again, it doesn't matter if you officially create a corporation to do your trades or not, it's still a business no matter what. That means you should approach things with care and avoid the get rich quick mentality. The fact is the get rich quick mentality never works anywhere. Unfortunately, I guess I could say I've been too strong in my assertion.

It does work on rare occasions. It works well enough that it keeps the myth alive. But if we took 100 Forex traders who have to get rich quick mentality, my bet is within 90 days, 95% of them would be completely broke.

- Trade Small

You should always trade small and set small achievable goals for your trading. The first benefit to trading small is that this approach will help you avoid a margin call. Second, it will also help you set profit goals that are small and achievable. That will help you stay in business longer.

Simply put, you will start gaining confidence and learning how to trade effectively if you get some trades that make $50 profits, rather than shooting for a couple of trades that would make thousands of dollars in one shot, but and up making you completely broke. Again, treat your trading like a real business. If you were opening a business, chances are you would start looking for slow and steady improvements and you certainly would not hope to get rich quick.

Let's get specific. Trading small means never trading standard lots. Even if you have enough cash to open an account such that you could trade standard lots, I highly recommend that you stay away from them. The large amount of capital involved and margin that would be used could just get you into a lot of financial trouble. For beginners, no matter how much money you are able to devote to your trading, I recommend that you start with micro lots. Take some time and learn how to trade with the small lots and start building your business earnings small profits at a time. Trading only with micro lots will help in force discipline and help you avoid getting into trouble. Make a commitment only to use micros for the first 60 days. After that, if you have been having decent success, consider trading a mini lot. You should be extremely cautious for the first 90 days in general.

- Be Careful with Leverage

Obviously, it's extremely beneficial. It allows you to enter and trades that would otherwise not be possible. On the other hand, the temptation is there to use all your leverage in the hopes of making it big on one or two trades. You need to avoid using up all your leverage. Remember that you can have a margin call and get yourself into big trouble if your trades go bad.

And it's important to remember there's a high probability that some of your trades are going to go bad no matter how carefully you do all your analysis.

- Not Using A Demo Account

A big mistake the beginners make, is jumping in too quickly. There is a reason that most broker-dealers provide demos or simulated accounts. If you don't have a clue what that reason is, let's go ahead and stated here. Brokers provide demo accounts because Forex is a high-risk trading activity. It can definitely be something that provides a lot of rewards and it does for large numbers of traders. But there is a substantial risk of losing your capital. Many beginners are impatient hoping to make money right away. That's certainly understandable, but you don't want to fall into that trap. Take 30 days to practice with a demo account. This will provide several advantages. Trading on Forex is different than trading on the stock market. Using the demo account, you can become familiar with all the nuances of Forex trading. This includes everything from studying the charts, to placing your orders and, most importantly, understanding both pips and margin. The fact that there is so much leverage available means you need to learn how to use it responsibly. You need to know how to experience going through the process and reading the available margin and so forth on your trading platform while you are actually trying to execute trades. A demo account let you do this without risking real capital. It is true that it's not a perfect simulation. The biggest argument against demo accounts is that they don't incorporate the emotion that comes with trading and real money. As we all know, it's those emotions, including panic, fear and greed, that lead to bad decisions. However, in my opinion, that is a weak argument against using demo accounts. The proper way to approach it is to use a demo account for 30 days and then spend 60 to 90 days doing nothing but trading micro lots. Don't worry, as your micro trading lots you can increase the number of your trades and earn profits. While I know you're anxious to get started, keeping yourself from losing all your money is a good reason to practice for 30 days before doing it for real.

- Failing to Check Multiple Indicators

There is also a temptation to get into trades quickly just on a gut level hunch. You need to avoid this approach at all costs. Some beginners will start learning about candlesticks and then when they first start trading, they will recognize a pattern on a chart. Then in the midst of the excitement, they will enter a large trade based on what they saw. And then they will end up on the losing end of a trade. Some people are even worse and they don't even look at the candlesticks. Instead, they just look at the trend and think they better get in on it and they got all anxious about doing so. That means first checking the candlesticks and then confirming at least with the moving average before entering or exiting a position. You should also have the RSI handy and you may or may not want to use Bollinger bands.

- Use Stop Loss and Take Profit Orders

Well, I hate to repeat myself yet again, but this point is extremely important. I am emphasizing it over and over because it's one of the tools that you can use in order to protect yourself from heavy losses. One of the ways that you can get out of having to worry about margin calls and running out of money is to put stop-loss orders every time you trade. This will require studying the charts more carefully. You need to have a very clear idea where you want to get out of the trade, if it doesn't go in the direction you hoped. But if you have a stop-loss order in place, then you can avoid the problem of having your account just go down the toilet. Secondly, although the temptation is always there to look for as many profits as possible, in most cases, you should opt to set a take profit order when you make your trade. That way you set as we said, distinct boundaries which will ensure that you make some profit without taking too much risk. The problem with doing it manually is that excitement and greed will put you in a position where are you miss the boat entirely. What inevitably happens, is people get too excited hoping to earn more profits and they stay in the trade too long. The Forex market changes very fast and so what eventually happens is people that stay in for too long inevitably end up with a loss. Or at the very least they end up missing out on profits.

There is one exception to this point. There are times when there is a distinct and relatively long-term upward trend. If you find yourself, by doing the analysis and determining that such an upward trend is here, that might be an exception to the rule. In that case you want to try to ride the trend and maximize your profits.

- Remember Price Changes Are in Pips

Beginners often make the mistake of forgetting about pips. If you have trouble with pips and converting them to actual money. Remember that pips play a central role in price changes, you need to know your dollar value per pip in order to keep tabs on your profit and losses. This is also important for knowing the right stop loss and take profit orders to execute.

- Don't Try Too Many Strategies or Trading Styles at Once

When you are a beginning Forex trader, it can be tempting to try everything under the sun. That can be too much for a lot of people. The most advisable thing to do is to stick with one strategy so don't try scalping and being a position trader at the same time. The shorter the time frame for your trades, the more time and energy, you have to put into each trade. Scalping and day trading are activities that would require full-time devotion. They are also high-pressure and that can help enhance emotions involved in the trades. For that reason, I don't really recommend those styles or strategies for beginners. In my opinion and to be honest it's mine alone, I think position trading is also too much for a beginner. It requires too much patience.

Perhaps the best strategy to use when you're beginning Forex trading is to become a swing trader. It's a nice middle ground, in between the most extremely active trading styles and something that is going to try people's patience such as position trading. When you do swing trading, you can do time periods longer than a day certainly, but as long or short as you need to meet your goals otherwise. Swing trading also takes off some of the pressure. And it gives you more time to think and react.

This does not mean that you can't become a scalper or day trader at some future date.

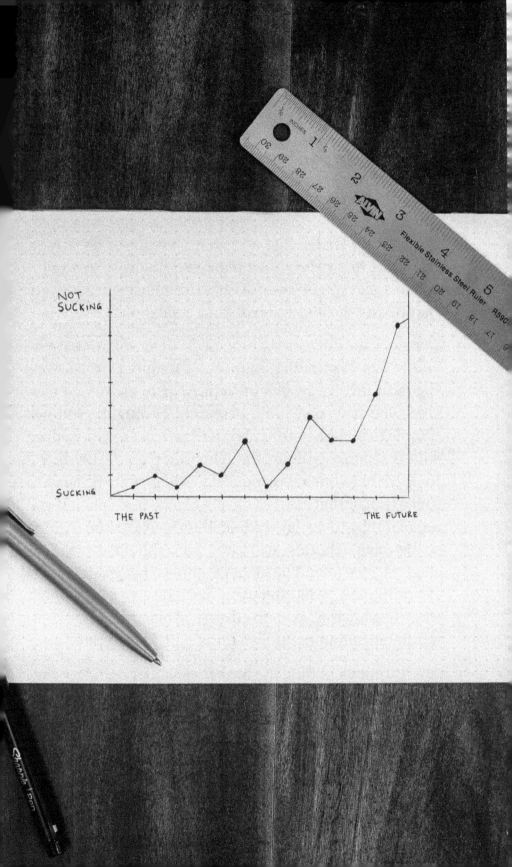

CHAPTER 6 - Trade Management and Position Sizing

The use of an effective management system for your money can begin to help you cultivate wins even if you only have 4 trades that are profitable out of the 10. So, take time to practice, then plan, and finally structure the threads that you do according to the management of your money and the allocation of your capital plan.

Consider the charges that the brokerage will be charging you. When day trading, you will see frequent transactions that will involve results of highly costly brokerage fees. Once you have done your research thoroughly, you will be able to plan the proper brokerage firm that you will go with through a carefully thought after plan. If you intend to only trade one or two per day, then you will need to find a broker that charges on a per trade basis plan. If you are planning to do day trading, then your volume is going to be high. In this instance, you should go with a staggered fee plan. The higher volumes that you have, the lower the cost will effectively be. You can also benefit from a plan that is a fixed rate. This will provide an unlimited amount of trades for one high fixed rate.

Apart from all of this, the broker also offers services that include utilities for trading, and platforms that you can utilize for trading. The integrated solution for trading can be things such as combinations options, software trading, data for historical accuracy, tools that help with research, alerts for the trades, applications that chart with indicators that are technical along with features that are not already listed. Some of these features can be cost-effective or free, while some may come with a cost that could eat a hole in your profits or wallet. You should pick the features that are handy for your trading needs and avoid the ones that are subscribed to help with specific needs. A novice can start with basic low-cost brokerage fees that match the trading needs that are initially set and then later they can opt for modules and upgrades that are needed at this time.

You will also need to be able to simulate or reverse test the historical data of the strategies and trading charts. Once you have set a plan and it is ready, then you need to be able to simulate it to test the strategy and utilize the test to run a virtual test account with virtual money. Many of the brokers that you can hire will allow you to run a test for your account. You can also use historical data to backtest the strategy. This will give you an assessment that is realistic, as well as keep considerations for the cost of the brokerage and fees that subsequently will come up for the various different utilities.

Strategies

For most people, strategies are used in businesses to give business operations a sense of direction. However, most people ignore the fact that strategies are an important part of our everyday lives. They enable you to live your life in order and achieve even the simplest of goals. Basically, any journey undertaken without a strategy does not have an actual blueprint for addressing the various elements of the journey.

The significance of workable strategies cannot be underestimated when it comes to day trading. They form the framework under which the market can be studied, and traders leverage the most lucrative chances of making profits. In all day trading strategies, there is a need for in-depth technical analysis to establish the patterns of the price movements through charts and the different indicators for different strategies. The basic tenet of a day trading strategy is that emotions should be out of the strategy development process. Every strategy chosen should be based on facts, and there are various factors to be considered when choosing any strategy.

Trading Based on the Time of Day

Often, this fundamental analysis is going to be saved for long-term investing, something that you don't see much with day traders. It takes into account how the price of the company will go into the future when compared to where it is now, but these changes are often going to occur over weeks, months, or even years. Day trading takes place in one day. Because of this, most day traders will not use this information to help them make decisions about which stocks to trade in.

As a day trader, you probably won't spend a lot of time working on fundamental research. Most traders know that demand for ethanol is going to make a difference in the price of corn during a particular time period. But day traders want to focus more on what the price is going to do right now compared to where it was a few minutes ago.

CHAPTER 7 - Binary Options

Binary options are similar to traditional options in many ways except that they ultimately boil down to a basic yes or no question. Instead of worrying about what exact price an underlying stock is going to have, a binary option only cares if it is going to be above one price at the time of its expiration. Traders then make their trades based on if they believe the answer is yes or no at which time it will be worth either $0 or $100. While it may seem simple on its face, it is important that you fully understand the ways in which binary options work, as well as the time frames and markets they work with. It is also important to understand the specific advantages and disadvantages that they have and which companies are legally allowed to offer binary options for trade.

If you are currently considering trading in binary options then it is also important to be aware that binary options trading outside of the US has a different structure. Also, when hedging or speculating, it is important to keep in mind that doing so is considered an exotic options trade so the rules are different still. Regardless, the price of a binary option is always going to be somewhere between $0 and $100, it is also going to come with a bid price as well as an ask price, just like any other type of option.

They are also a great way for those who are interested in day-trading but don't have the serious capital required to get off the ground, to ply their trade.

Traditional stock day trading limits don't apply with binary options so you are allowed to start trading with just 1, $100 deposit. It is also important to keep in mind that binary options are a derivative created by its association with an underlying asset which means they don't give you ownership of that asset in any way. As such you would be unable to exercise them as a means of generating dividends or utilizing voting rights.

The Benefits of Picking Binary Options

Some of the benefits you will notice with using binary options instead of another investment includes:

The potential for a high return: this is a risky form of investing, but if you learn to read the market properly, you will find that it has a lot of potential for a lot of money to come to you. If you do well with this trading option, you could see a return on investment between 60 to 90 percent.

The risk is fixed: You will know right at the beginning how much money you stand to lose or to win depending on which way the prediction goes. This helps make it easier to decide on your choices. Other investments can end up being a lot of guesswork and if things go south, you can lose a lot more than you put into the whole thing. On the other hand, with binary options, you know exactly how much you stand to gain and lose right off the top.

You can even win after losing: Since you will find that the risks on these options are high, there are some brokers that offer a return on money that you invested if your predictions were wrong. This is not going to be the full amount but getting a small percentage of your money back can be encouraging compared to losing it all.

Easy trading: These are easier to trade on. Other options in the stock market make this hard, but the platforms for binary options help the investor trade without all the hassle. You can work with a live chat feature to do this or even with your broker if you have some questions. In addition, there are really only two options for most of your trading options so this makes things easier as well.

Rewards: The risk associated with any binary option is always going to cap out at the cost of the initial trade because the worst result for any option is for it to time out and be worth $0. The reward is also capped and based on the amount of the initial investment. As an example, if you purchase a $20 binary option then you are always going to make $100 at most, which means you will make $80 and have a 4:1 risk/reward ration which is better than you will find in most other situations most of the time.

This will only be in your benefit for a limited time, however, as gains will never increase pass $100 regardless of how much movement an underlying asset may have. The easiest way to mitigate this particular downside is to simply double down on options contracts from the start.

How to Trade Binary Options

Binary options are currently traded on the Nadex exchange which was the first exchange created expressly to sell binary options in the United States. It offers market access as well as its own trading platform which always has access to the most recent binary options pricing.

It is also possible to trade options on the Chicago Board Options Exchange which can be accessed by those with an options trading approved brokerage account through more traditional means. When doing so, it is important to keep in mind that not all brokers are going to offer options trading which means that if this is a route you are considering going down you will need to plan accordingly and choose your broker with these services in mind.

Trading via Nadex costs 90 cents per trade with a maximum fee of $9 per transaction which means that lots greater than 10 are essentially free. The fee is not deducted from the trading account until the trade has expired and if the trade does not end profitably then there is no charge as well. Trading on the Chicago Board is subject to traditional brokerage fees.

Choosing the right market: There is nothing stopping you from trading across various asset classes at once when it comes to binary options and, indeed, Nadex allows trading across most of the major indices including the S&P 500, Nasdaq 100, Russell 2000 and the Dow 30. Available global indices include those from the UK, Germany, and Japan. Trades are also available for a variety of forex pairs including AUD/JPY, EUR/GBP, USD/CHF, GBP/JPY, USD/CAD, AUD/USD, EUR/JPY, USD/JPY, GBP/UDS, and EUR/USD.

Another popular option through Nadex is the commodity binary options which include crude oil, natural gas, gold, copper, silver, corn, and soybeans. There are also several options when it comes to trading based on a specific news event which means you can buy options on things like if the Federal Reserve is going to decide to decrease or increase the joblessness claims percentage or if the nonfarm payroll ends up beating its current estimates.

The Chicago Board offers a smaller selection of binary options overall, but those that it does offer are not available anywhere else. For example, it is only there where you can find binary options based on numerous interpretations of the S&P 500 or a volatility index based on its very own volatility index.

Binary Option Timeframes

Weekly Trading: Weekly binary options are listings that provide the opportunity for trading in the short-term along with lots of opportunities to hedge the choices you do make. As you might infer from the name, weekly trading means working with options that expire in exactly one week with the standard being for them to be listed on Thursday and expire the next Friday. While this type of binary options trading has been around for quite some time, they were largely only used by investors who followed the cash indices. This exclusivity has changed in the past decade as the Chicago Board has started expanding the practice of this type of trading until now there are nearly 1,000 opportunities to do so each week.

Beyond just having a specific timeframe, weekly binary options are different than more traditional options in that they can only be purchased 21 days out of the month which is why they aren't listed as expiring in the monthly style. As such, in the week that monthly options are set to expire, they are technically classified as weekly options.

The biggest benefit with this type of binary option is that it makes it extremely easier to purchase exactly what you are looking for in a specific trade without needing to come up with additional capital just to end up with more than you actually need. For those who are interested in selling, weekly binary options make it easier to do so more regularly as opposed to having to wait a month or more between sales.

Weekly binary options trades are also worth considering in that they ultimately lead to lower costs for trades with larger spreads like calendar or diagonal spreads as you can sell weekly binary options against them in the interim. They also come in handy when it comes to higher volumes of trades overall, especially when it comes to hedging larger positions in risky markets. Likewise, if the market is range bound the weekly market will still be fruitful thanks to strategies like the iron condor or iron butterfly.

The biggest downside to weekly binary options is that you won't have much of a chance of things changing in your favor if you choose poorly from the start. Likewise, if you are looking to short the binary option in question then it is important to keep in mind that it would only take a relatively small overall move to push something into the money.

It is also important to keep in mind that these types of options require even more micromanaging than most which means that if you do not take the time to size up your trades properly as a means of guaranteeing profits you will find that your total trade balance starts to drop quite sharply. Along similar lines, the implied volatility for each trade is going to be higher than would otherwise be the case because of the shorten timeframe that you are dealing with. Near term options will always be subject to bigger swings as well.

As you will have less time with which to turn a profit when dealing with weekly binary options when you do make a move it is vital that your timing is as precise as possible as if you choose poorly then you can easily find yourself paying for something that will end up being worthless practically as soon as you put your money down. It is also important to consider how much risk the option offers as buying in bulk is always cheaper if you have the data to back it up.

Along similar lines, it is important to avoid naked puts or calls when trading in the weekly timeframe as these often end up with a lower probability of success overall. If you are quite specific when it comes to the directions of your chosen trades then a structured trade or a debit spread may be a better choice.

CHAPTER 8 - Swing Trading Options

An alternative is a money related subordinate. It is a real agreement that gives the purchaser the option to purchase or sell a security at a specific date (the activity date). The merchant furthermore holds a promise to fulfill the trade, which is to purchase or sell, if the purchaser rehearses the choice before its end. The purchasing and selling of investment opportunities is controlled by the US securities and trade commission.

Numerous procedures are utilized by the individuals who trade alternatives. Every one of them anyway includes either purchasing or selling at least one choice. They do this in heading or unbiased reaction to showcase see on the underlying resource.

They ordinarily utilize uncommonly arranged diagrams called alternative 'payout or result profiles' to get a pictorial perspective on what the procedure will yield more gains on its 'running-out' date for an assortment of unique sell esteems, for example, the one demonstrated as follows.

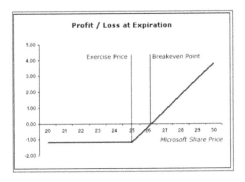

From the diagram over, the line shows the way wherein the trade will come into benefit if the market goes past the make back the initial investment point. In any case, the chart doesn't show that a merchant can take benefit by shutting the trade before its lapse. This is conceivable when you can sell the choice for more than you got it. This is commonly the target when swing trading choices.

In case you're not effectively acquainted with Options trading, presently would be a decent time to do some examination.

The swing trading Options technique has three primary advantages:

- Profit age
- Limited hazard presentation
- You can trade significant expense stocks with an extremely little record.

The general techniques with regards to alternatives trading are the call and put choices. The call choice initiates an acquisition of stocks while the put alternatives show an interest in selling a stock.

It is moderately simple to figure out how to swing trade alternatives since it is a directional technique for the market. The stunts underneath will give you a thought of a straightforward technique for swing trading choices. At the point when you become familiar with this, you can adjust it to as you advance your aptitudes. Swing trading alternatives isn't entangled. It offers a course to more make sure about benefits than most systems.

Here are five stages to comprehend swing trading for Options in its most basic components

Step 1: How to Select the Right Stocks

Regardless of how ingenious your system is, on the off chance that you are trading an inappropriate stock, you would wind up blowing through your record. Choosing the correct stock can be overwhelming when you don't have the foggiest idea what you are searching for seeing as there are handfuls recorded on the major exchange markets. A basic method to begin is to have a part watch list that you work with the main stocks on the planet. At that point you watch this rundown for enormous moves in order to pick the correct contender for your system. The way to choose those with the biggest moves as you need to exploit the value swings. You can go above and beyond to check the reason for this huge rate development in cost. If it is brought about by essential variables, it improves the stock a competitor.

Step 2: How to Assess the Market

Each market will be in a specific state when you enter. You should guarantee to check the history and, if conceivable, use devices (like the Bollinger groups) to survey the market to discover what state it is in. The market can either be in a pattern (upturn or downtrend) or not (going sideways). In the event that the market is in a pattern, you need to figure out which sort of pattern and the quality of the pattern. For an upward pattern, you are searching for 'higher highs' and 'higher lows.' For a descending pattern you are looking for lower lows and lower highs. You should remember that you should consistently go with the pattern. When there is an upturn, pick just call choices. When in a downtrend, pick just put choices. A significant evaluation you should make next is the unpredictability in the market. It is ideal to go to little time spans (5 mins, 10 mins, and 60 minutes) to check this. Realizing the unpredictability will assist you with settling on the lapse of your trade.

Step 3: Decide Your Entry

This is perhaps the most significant choice to make on the grounds that a couple of pips could have a significant effect. This is the place acceptable information on specialized and essential investigation comes to play. These are shrouded later. For the most part, the section cost is the point that you are wagering the cost will go over or underneath at the termination time.

Step 4: How to Select an Expiration time

Specialized investigation is the particular most significant decider of the decision of the lapse to pick. The decision of termination relies exclusively upon the time span that specialized investigation was made. For the most part, while doing specialized examination, brokers regularly utilize diverse time spans to get by and large and explicit thought of the market development. Be that as it may, when deciding on a trade, there is the base time allotment whereupon significant investigation is completed. You need to utilize products of this time allotment while picking a termination. For example, if the TA is done on a brief diagram, your time lapse ought to be 15 minutes, 30 minutes, 45 minutes, 60minutes... in a specific order. This makes your expectations simpler.

By and large, numerous dealers offer the best yields on the most limited terminations (30 secs, 1 moment). In any case, these courses of events forecast the most elevated hazard levels. The more extended the expiration, the lesser the hazard and the lesser the prize. I will encourage you to favor the month to month time allotment since this will take into account not so much risk but rather more precise TA.

Step 5: Manage the Trade

On the off chance that you happen to enter the market during times of low instability what you ought to do is to sell your choice before its terminations. Alternatives experience what is known as time rot. This essentially the decrease in the estimation of choice as the approaches its lapse. For example, an alternative worth $30 at its buy for 10 minutes when out of the cash may drop to about $ 29.50 in the initial 2 minutes and drop similarly as $2 in the eighth moment. In the event that it is in cash, the rate gain drops additionally as it arrives at its lapse should you decide to sell it. It can drop from an underlying 85% to 60%. It is shrewd to sell immediately when out of the cash or in the cash in the event that you don't confide later on for the alternatives. Swing trading alternatives can be a ground-breaking technique when aced. This needs a ton of practice and perseverance. Numerous alternatives dealers will in general need to make easy money. Along these lines, they trade exceptionally little league outlines. Swing merchants don't.

CHAPTER 9 - Options on Index Funds

One of the most popular index funds that is used is called SPY, namely for the S&P 500.

For those who don't know, an exchange-traded fund is basically a mutual fund that trades like a stock. Investment companies collect a large amount of money, and then they buy shares in multiple companies. So, in the case of SPY, the fund owns shares in all 500 companies on the index. A large amount of money has to be assembled to make those kinds of investments.

Try and imagine if you wanted to invest in every single company that belongs to the S&P 500 or the Dow Jones industrial average. That would be quite a daunting task and unless you are a billionaire, it might even be impossible. But you could imagine trying to buy shares in each individual stock. Let's stick with the S&P 500 as an example. That would mean that you would have to pick out the 500 companies and buy shares in each one of them. Chances are not good for you to get very far in this task.

And then you have to take into account that this is not a static list of companies. That is, it will be changing with time. Companies can be removed from the list and new ones added as up and coming corporations replace others.

Therefore, it makes sense to leave such a project to professionals who have a lot of money to invest. So far it sounds like I have made a great argument for a mutual fund. And I suppose that mutual funds do have their advantages. For starters, we know that such funds automatically give you a diverse portfolio. Also, a professional money manager would attempt to build a portfolio with a higher probability of success, there would be a possibility that his or her fund would actually perform better than the S&P 500 index itself. This is in fact, what professional money managers try to attempt with these funds. Instead of putting equal investments in each of the S&P 500 companies, what they will do is put a little bit more money in high growth companies and a little bit less in companies that are stable or even in decline.

Of course, while mutual funds have their advantages for people that are planning for retirement and so forth, they might be boring for people who are inclined to be traders, rather than safety-oriented long-term investors. And there is a good reason for this. One thing to note about mutual funds is that they don't trade on the stock market. They only trade once a day after the market close. Also, mutual funds are well-known for having high expenses. In fact, in case you didn't know, the expenses associated with mutual funds are a bit notorious if they have loads.

Exchange-traded funds were developed with the idea of taking the advantages of mutual funds but without the disadvantages. So, the first major difference between an exchange-traded fund and a mutual fund is that the exchange-traded fund is traded actively on the stock market. Consider the following scenario. Exchange-traded funds trade just like a stock during the day.

So, if the S&P 500 index was going up strongly, you could check the price of the exchange-traded fund, and you may want to get in action. This way you could buy your shares there and then, or at the right moment as the case may be. But you cannot do this in quite the same way for a mutual fund. You could go ahead and submit an order during the day, but your order won't execute until the mutual fund trades at the end of the day. That means you really cannot be sure what price you are going to get. In contrast, an investor buying shares in an exchange-traded fund knows the exact price, just like anyone buying stock live does.

The second major advantage for exchange-traded funds over mutual funds is that they have very low expenses in comparison. So, the cost of investing in an exchange-traded fund as compared to a mutual fund that tracks the same index is going to be a lot lower.

For these reasons, many exchange-traded funds have become very popular. This is an excellent way for people to invest with diversification. So rather than having to deal with some fancy mutual fund with a bunch of polished publications, that are supposed to make you feel good about all the fees that they are charging you, you can simply sign on to your brokerage account and buy shares of an exchange-traded fund whenever you feel like it.

The popularity of these exchange-traded funds has had a big impact on options as well. Before the advent of exchange-traded funds, the only thing you could do with options was to buy them for regular stocks, but nowadays you can buy options in all kinds of different ways and for different types of investments. One of the most popular is the SPY, which we mentioned earlier. If you look at the SPY options, the level of activity as reflected in the volume and open interest is quite large when compared to that for individual stocks.

When you are buying and selling options in this case what you are doing is simply betting on the direction that the S&P 500 will go. Now that will not save you from making the wrong bets from time to time. No matter what, investing is always risky. And when you are talking about the stock market indices themselves, they are going to be more sensitive to external events, such as the government slapping on a new tariff, or if some political event causes an uproar.

This said, remember that, with options, one of the advantages is that we can find profit no matter which way the index moves.

Another great thing about the SPY is that the prices are relatively affordable. The share price of the index fund at the writing time is around $289 dollars a share. This is actually quite a nice price point. So, it is roughly about 10% of what the S&P 500 index is.

It is a good price point because higher prices make it easier to make profits. To make profits on low priced stocks like AMD you have to buy more options, which means less liquidity. At the other end of the spectrum, we have brands like Amazon, which of course is quite expensive, even for options.

So, let's look at a slightly out of the money option that expires in two weeks, so that we can get an idea of what the prices are going to be if we decided to purchase an option. A $289 strike call option which is slightly out of the money, is priced at $1.53. If you remember that options are a hundred shares, which is the price per share, so we could buy this option for $153.

This is a good strategy for when the market is going up. Small changes can mean big money. I, myself, made a recent trade buying some slightly out of the money call options for this exchange-traded fund, SPY.

Of course, we have to be aware that the opposite is possible too, but that is why a smart investor is a diversified investor. In the case of options that means if you are not using some of these strategies that lead to profits you are at least buying both call and put options, so that you can profit from different price movements. And, obviously, you are paying close attention to what is going on in the world, so that you are ready to sell when necessary.

The thing with options for exchange-traded funds is not just that you can invest in something great like SPY. There are exchange-traded funds for virtually anything under the sun, and since they are listed as stocks, you can trade options on them.

As another example, we can consider the exchange-traded fund GLD. In short, what this exchange-traded fund does is that it allows people to invest in gold. But the difference here is that you are not really investing in gold in the sense of going to buy a bar or nugget that you keep in a safe in your house. Instead what you are doing is buying into a fund that owns interests in gold, but trading it as if it was a stock. Well, actually, of course, the fund itself is a stock.

So, we can trade options on Gold without having to do anything special or go on commodities markets, you can simply do this on the stock market. Now, I haven't personally invested in this one; I am just mentioning it as an example of the variety of investment opportunities that exist when you start considering exchange-traded funds.

Gold is not the only other opportunity that is out there. One interesting twist to investing would be to consider an exchange-traded fund that invested in bonds. There are a wide variety of exchange-traded funds that invest in bonds. One of the most famous of these is JNK. This one actually invests in junk bonds. Now if you don't know what those are, I will briefly say that those are bonds issued by companies that have bad credit. Just like people with bad credit, they have to pay high interest rates. So, imagine if you have bad credit and you try buying a car. You will have to pay a ridiculously high-interest rate. The same principle applies to companies issuing bonds because a bond is the same as borrowing money.

So, a company with bad credit is going to be forced to pay high-interest rates on its bonds. So, although there is some risk in principle, you would be earning a really high-interest rate in return for taking that risk with your capital.

The advantage of an exchange-traded fund is that you are covered a little bit by the fact that you are investing in the exchange-traded fund rather than directly in the bonds themselves. So, while a company that may go bust in part underlies the exchange-traded fund, the people that manage the fund are buying and selling the bonds in order to keep the fund performing well. So, you don't really have to worry about some company defaulting on paying their bonds interest payments.

So, this could be another possibility for options trading. Again, this is not something I personally invested in, so I cannot say offhand whether or not this particular fund is profitable. The point of this exercise is to illustrate again the wide diversity of investment opportunities and that exchange-traded funds provide not only long-term investors, but people that might be interested in doing some unconventional business with the options.

Let's look at a few more possibilities. One example is that you can invest in foreign markets through exchange-traded funds. This means that rather than trying to invest overseas, you could buy options on exchange-traded funds that tracked high-growth companies in India or Russia for example.

CHAPTER 10 - Trading with LEAPS

Leaps are interesting options. They expire a year or more into the future. This is different than the short-term options that most people are trading. LEAPS are more expensive, but they can also represent money-making opportunities. LEAPS also give you an indirect way to control stock.

Profiting from LEAPS

LEAPS have high prices because they have a lot of extrinsic value. Looking at June 18, 2021, Facebook call options, the $195 call is priced at $42.13 a share. So that represents a $4,213 options contract. According to the chart, it made 3.4% today, which isn't a huge amount, but I challenge you to find a bank or mutual fund that has a return of 3.4% per day. The open interest is 133. This meets our minimum criteria for getting involved in a trade. It's quite small compared to Facebook options that expire in the next month, but it's enough open interest that it's going to be possible to get in and out of a trade in a reasonable amount of time. The implied volatility is a solid 33%. For comparison, the $195 call that expires in three weeks is priced at $12.48.

Although LEAPS are expensive, they have a lot of potential for profits. You can get into a LEAP and if the stock makes a solid move, you can close your position and make large amounts of money. For that $195 call that expires in June 2021, the delta is 0.64. That means that even though the option has a lot of extrinsic value since it expires a long way into the future, it's pretty sensitive to price changes in the stock that is with the option. If the share price goes up to $1, the option price will go up by $64. LEAPS don't suffer much from time decay. Theta for this option is only 0.03. If the share price goes up to $20 after an earnings call, the option is going to go up by $1,280. So you can make pretty good profits. The barrier to entry is the high price to buy one.

Poor Mans Covered Call

One of the interesting things that you can do with a LEAP is you can use it to sell covered calls. That sounds crazy, but it works. You can use the LEAP to cover call options that you sell to open. So you can invest in LEAPS at a fraction of what it costs to actually invest in the stock, and then start selling calls against the options to generate income. Although it might cost $4,600 to buy a Facebook LEAP, it would cost nearly $20,000 to buy 100 shares of stock. Buying a LEAP gives you de facto control over a hundred shares of stock at a much smaller price than the investment cost.

For the price of 100 shares of Facebook, you could invest in 4-5 LEAPS, and have a lot more room to work with as far as selling call options. So you could end up having a higher income.

CHAPTER 11 - Build A Trading Plan

You need to have a long-term plan of success that will serve as your reference guide, as well as a business plan.

Trading Plans

You'll hear a lot of trading gurus tell you to make a plan. Well, what exactly is a trading plan, and why do you need one? To be honest, a trading plan by itself is not going to matter too much. However, when done right, it can help you focus and really nail down your vision when it comes to trading.

Perhaps a more appropriate term for this is to call it a trading business plan instead of just a trading plan. Much like how you need to record all key information (both financial and in terms of vision) in your business plan, your trading plan needs to do the same for your trading business. At a minimum, it needs to have the following information.

Instruments to Trade

What instruments will you be trading? List them all out here. You can even take this a step further and list out the individual stocks you will be trading. When starting out, it's best to pick a single instrument and trade just that.

This doesn't mean you go out and try to trade everything under the sun.

You build a base with one, then two instruments, and then expand outward. Much like individuals, stocks have natures of their own in terms of liquidity and volatility. Some stocks have certain tendencies, depending on the time of the day.

You need to observe and learn all this in order to trade successfully, and doing so one by one is the way to go about it.

Markets and Timing

Which markets will you be trading? When will you trade them? Most of you reading this will have full-time jobs or something else going on. So, it is important for you to note down your session time and stick to it.

Which is the best session for beginners or busy people to trade? Well, there's no such thing as "best" to begin with. In terms of liquidity and best bang for your buck, the open is probably the best. The flip side to this is that the volatility can be pretty extreme. Things pick up toward the end of the day as well, so it's not as if the open is the only worthwhile time to trade.

The afternoon session is usually seen as something of a graveyard with a lot of traders stepping out for lunch. Don't just assume this is so. Observe the market and check its tendencies. While the more active stocks tend to slow down quite a bit, there are some instruments that provide easy pickings.

Capital and Risk per Trade

List out your trading capital and your risk per trade. You should not be risking more than 0.25% of your capital per trade, ideally 0.1%. If this reduced amount is too less for you to buy or sell any stock, then focus on getting more capital to start instead of increasing your risk per trade.

Risk Limits

What is your daily risk limit? Weekly, monthly, etc.? It is also a good idea to execute a gain-protection plan. What this means is that if you have a bunch of winners during the session (say two or more) or if you make a certain percentage of your account during the session (say anything about 0.5%), then you could decide to stop trading during that session if your gains dip below 0.25% or if you lose two more trades.

The idea is that you've made money during the session and you would like to hang on to it. This is to protect a string of winners or a huge gain. Once you've had a great day, it's perfectly fine to set a lower loss limit in order to protect some of it so that no matter what happens, you'll end the day up.

CHAPTER 12 - Risk in Options Trading

Risk is at the heart of all types of investment as without it there would be need for reward. As such, options trading is risky at the best of times, even for those who might be considered experts and certainly for those who are still new to the field. Luckily, there are certainly ways to mitigate that risk as many of the major pitfalls of options trading have been well documented by those who have come before. What's more, they have also been distilled down and classified so that all you need to do is memorize the following and ensure that you do your best to not let it intrude on your trading success.

It doesn't matter what type of trade you are working with, the first thing you are going to want to do is to take three main things into consideration. First, you will want to be aware of how much a specific price is likely going to change prior to the expiration of the option in question. From there, you will want to determine how volatile the underlying asset is as well as how much time the option has to turn you a profit prior to its expiration. When you are purchasing options, it is important to also identify the direction you expect the underlying stock to move in as well as how long you expect it to continue to move in the specified direction. In these instances, the amount of time that is still available won't be as important when it comes to ensuring the overall maximum value.

To ensure that you minimize risk, it is important to keep in mind that the best strategies are those that focus on either high positive risk value or high negative risk value, there is little value in betting on the middle ground. Remember, some option types are always going to end up being more profitable than others in specific scenarios, you just need to have the patience and the foresight to know what's coming before it gets here. With that being said, however, it is important to always keep in mind that statistical projections cannot actually tell the future which means that any analysis that is done is strictly hypothetical. Never invest more money into a particular trade, no matter how reliable it seems, than you can ultimately afford to lose.

When it comes to making trades in groups, or combining them in other ways, it is important to consider the net risk of the entire trade instead of focusing on the specific risk likelihoods of parts of the whole. This will make it easier for you to determine the most profitable way to move forward at any juncture because it makes the risk/reward split much easier to analyze. Remember, there are multiple different types of risk which means that understanding what each means for your specific trade is crucial to covering all your bases and making success options trades on a reliable basis.

Delta:

Delta can be thought of as the amount of overall risk that you take on depending on how likely the underlying asset in question is going to move prior to the point where the option expires. If the asset is at the money at the moment then the delta is going to be .5. What you can take from this is the fact that when the underlying asset moves a single point in either direction then the option will move .5 points. Puts are always going to have a delta of somewhere between -1 and 0 and calls will always have a delta that is somewhere between 1 and 0.

Delta should always be the first type of risk that you consider as it will do the most to help you immediately determine if a specific trade is going to be in your best interest or not. You will find that it is the most helpful when it can be used to make decisions related to puts you are interested in making as it will help make it clear the direction the underlying asset is going to be likely to move in. To determine the delta, you are going to want to start by considering historical data related to the underlying assets by looking at previous strike prices in comparison to their comparable puts. When it comes to measuring delta, it is important to keep in mind that cheaper options are naturally going to have a lower delta. This occurs naturally as delta measures the chance an option will be profitable at expiration. This is why you are going to always want to avoid options with a delta that is either .4 or -.4 because it is rather unlikely that they are going to end up being favorable trades by the time everything is said and done.

Rho:

Rho is the name given to the quantity of risk that surrounds the interest rates relating to an underlying asset and the probably that changes in this area will result in changes to the underlying asset price and thus negatively affect the price of the option as well. As a general rule, you can expect interest rates to increase along with call prices, causing a decrease in put values. The reverse of this statement will also be true, causing an increase in put prices and a decrease in interest rates. Rho is going to be the most influential when the price of the underlying asset is greater than or equal to the option price. Calls will always have a positive Rho and puts will always have a negative rho. Rho is going to be relevant primarily those who are interested in options trading as a form of long-term investment.

Gamma:

If delta measures the amount of change that occurs between the underlying asset and the option in question, then gamma measures the likelihood that the delta is going to remain the same as long as the option remains active. The larger the gamma grows, the closer the underlying asset and the related option are likely to be to one another and a smaller gamma means that the variation between them is quite large because the stock has fallen beneath the strike point. Big gammas mean big profits but also larger degrees of risk. Additionally, you will want to keep in mind that the gamma will increase naturally as it gets closer to the point at which the option is going to expire. If you need to know just how much the gamma is likely to increase during this period you can certainly find out, all you need to do is consider the gamma of the gamma.

Theta:

Theta is a representation of the rate at which the time the option has left is currently expiring in comparted to how much time it has as a whole. Theta starts as a positive amount that starts to tick down the instant that an option comes into existence. Theta decreases at a steady rate compared to the price of the related option as it is guaranteed to lose value each second it ticks closer to expiration. A trade will remain profitable for the holder as long as delta remains greater than theta and will make money for the writer once this balance reverses itself.

As an options trader, it is important to always be aware of the fact that theta will constantly be changing, and that this change will increase in frequency the closer the option it is measuring gets to its expiration point. Theta is going to be the most important variable to consider if you are planning to make a trade based around the assumption that the market is not going to change prior to the options expiration. If this is not the case, then theta will be the least relevant element of risk to your trades as long as you work around it as needed.

Vega:

Vega is the type of risk that measure how volatile the underlying asset is compared to the market as a whole. Vega can be difficult to accurately determine at points, simply because it is possible to change despite the fact that the price of the asset it points to remained neutral during the same period. As such, making a successful options trade doesn't mean being able to avoid vega completely, it means understanding how to take advantage of it regardless of the level of volatility that is in play.

Different options are going to respond in different ways to increasing vega; those that respond positively are known as long volatility options and those that respond negatively are called short volatility options. Options that have a long volatility will have a positive amount of vega and short volatility options are going to have a mega vega. If you find an option with a neutral vega then it will have a neutral level of volatility to go along with it.

CHAPTER 13 - Tips for Success

Stay away from calls that are Out of the Money: If a call is not at least at the money then it is not worth your time. While you have likely heard the old adage, buy low and sell high, that is never the right choice in this case as calls that are out of the money are much less likely to get back to where they need to be if you hope to turn a profit on them. This, in turn, amounts to little more than gambling because there are always going to be relatively few indicators that you can rely on to determine if the price is going to stabilize in the time allotted.

It is important to keep in mind that buying an option means knowing what direction an underlying stock is going to move in, but it is just as important to know when it is going to move in that direction. If you misjudge either, then you are likely to lose out on the commission in addition to not being able to use that money in other more profitable ways until the option expires. Don't forget, in order to make money you need the option to increase all the way from out of the money to the strike price if you want to make a profit.

Work Out Multiple Strategies: Eventually you will start to feel constrained by the system or plan that you are utilizing and want to expand into a wider variety of options. When this happens it is important that you work out new plans and strategies instead of trying to force your existing strategy to work in ways that it was not designed to. Certain strategies are always only going to work in certain scenarios and trying to force them to do otherwise is just asking for trouble. What's worse, these faulty decisions are going to taint your overall trade average, making your plan seem worse than it actually is.

Utilize a Spread: A long spread is comprised of a pair of options, one with a higher cost and the other with a lower cost. The higher cost option is the one that you will buy and the other is the one that you will sell. Everything about the pair of options should be the same except for their strike prices. When using a spread, it is important that you always keep the time value in mind or else you will find yourself in a scenario where it serves to limit your profits.

Always be clear on when you will be entering or exiting: Ensuring that you know exactly when you want to start a trade or to exit an existing trade can become more difficult the more your emotions begin to come into play. While it will be difficult to leave money on the table at first, having limits to your trade will keep you from losing much more money than it will ultimately cost you. What's more, when you think about the amount of money that you are likely to gain in the short period between when you should exit a trade and when you ultimately do, the amount saved is typically going to be negligible.

Don't Double Up: If a trade that appears as though it is going to turn a profit suddenly and unexpectedly moves in the wrong direction, the reaction of many novice options traders is going to be let emotion get the better of you and possibly double down on what is rapidly becoming a bad investment in hopes of making back all of the money that was previously lost. If you find yourself in a situation where you are thinking about doubling down on something questionable you can keep yourself from making the wrong decision by first asking yourself if you would have made the decision if things had gone your way from the start. In nearly all scenarios, cutting your losses and moving forward with a clear head is the preferable action. Remember, there are always more profitable trades on the horizon.

Keep Earnings Dates in Mind: When it comes to maximizing your earning potential, it is important to have a clear idea of when any of the underlying stocks related to your options are going to have to disclose their earnings for the past quarter. Regardless of what the outcome of these calls is going to be, they are sure to generate a fair amount of movement when it comes to the stock in question which means being caught unaware can leave you trading based on information that is suddenly extremely outdated. Option prices typically tend to spike around earnings time as a result.

Additionally, it is important to keep in mind when any underlying stock is going to be paying dividends as well. This is extremely important because unless you exercise the options related to the stocks that are going to be paying dividends then you won't make any money in the process. These dividends can sometimes be assigned earlier than expected which is why you always want to have a firm grasp on the newest information available regarding the dates in question.

Understand The Risk Of Early Assignment: It is common for new traders to sell options or months without realizing they are putting themselves at risk until they are handed their first early assignment and are forced to deal with it in any way possible. The early assignment occurs when a holder exercises their rights well before the expiration date of the option in question that you are the writer on and it means you have to fulfill your obligation even if the terms aren't as much in your favor as you would like. If this happens to you the best thing you can do is not to let your emotions get the better of you and instead look for ways to make the best of a bad situation before committing to anything specific.

Commit to Spreads Only When Appropriate: When you are first starting out it can be easy to start a spread, consider all available options and then setting up the remainder of the spread. If you typically find yourself buying a call, finding the best possible moment, and then setting up a sell call then you will likely find yourself in a situation where a sudden change of fortune between the two makes seeing even a marginal return on your investment more difficult than you previously intended. This can easily be presented by committing to a spread all at once as this will provide fewer chances for various variables to sneak in and ruin your calculations.

Trade What You Can Afford to Lose: One of the most difficult lessons for many new options traders to learn is that you must never put more into a trade than you can realistically afford to lose, regardless of how good of a deal the trade appears to be at the time. There is never, ever going to be a trade that is a sure thing which means that luck will always play a factor no matter how airtight your system may have appeared to be in the past. If you typically take bigger risks than you can realistically afford, it isn't a question of if you will learn your lesson, it is a matter of when.

CONCLUSION

Congratulations on making it to the end of the book. I hope that thanks to my advice you are passionate about these businesses and that you have learned everything you need to become a master of your sector. As in everything, in this business it takes patience, intelligence and information. I gave you the information you need in this book, now it's up to you to have the tenacity to pursue your goal and achieve your goal of earning money with this business. I hope you will work hard and get maximum results in a short time.

Good luck.

CPSIA information can be obtained
at www.ICGtesting.com
Printed in the USA
BVHW092019010621
608472BV00002B/325